OCEANS

Troll Associates

OCEANS

by Francene Sabin

Illustrated by June Goldsborough

Troll Associates

Library of Congress Cataloging in Publication Data

Sabin, Francene.
  Oceans.

  Summary: A brief introduction to the characteristics
of the Earth's oceans.
    1. Oceanography—Juvenile literature.   [1. Oceanogra-
phy]   I. Goldsborough, June, ill.   II. Title.
GC21.5.S22   1985   551.46   84-8590
ISBN 0-8167-0216-0 (lib. bdg.)
ISBN 0-8167-0217-9 (pbk.)

Copyright © 1985 by Troll Associates, Mahwah, New Jersey
All rights reserved. No part of this book may be used
or reproduced in any manner whatsoever without written
permission from the publisher.
Printed in the United States of America

10   9   8   7   6   5   4   3   2   1

The blue-green waters stretch out all the way to the distant horizon. White-capped waves crash against the rocky shore, sending a fine spray of frothy foam high into the air. Farther out, large swells of water rise and fall like an endless roller coaster. The water is cold and salty and deep. This is the ocean. It is home for millions of living things, both small and large, both common and uncommon.

More than two thirds of the Earth's surface is covered by water. A small amount of that water is in the form of freshwater lakes, ponds, rivers, and streams. But most of it is salt water in the world's oceans and seas. The main difference between oceans and seas is size. Oceans are larger than seas.

There are five oceans on the Earth. They

Atlantic Ocean

Pacific Ocean

are the Atlantic, the Pacific, the Indian, the Arctic, and the Antarctic. Sometimes the Arctic and Antarctic Oceans are said to be parts of the other oceans. And sometimes all the oceans are thought of as being one huge body of water—often called the World Ocean.

Arctic Ocean

Indian Ocean

Antarctic Ocean

Oceans seem to have been here forever—but they haven't been. When this planet was first formed, it was an incredibly hot mass of liquid rock and gas. The heat sent up huge clouds of water vapor into the atmosphere. Then, over millions of years, the Earth and its atmosphere cooled.

Some scientists think the water vapor fell back to the Earth as rain, forming great bodies of fresh water in low-lying areas. Other scientists believe the water was released from the rocks themselves as they cooled and became solid. The water ran into low-lying areas and formed freshwater oceans.

Gradually, the freshwater oceans became saltier and saltier. Some of the salt came from the land. Some of the salt came from coastal soil and rocks that were worn away by wind and rain, and washed into the oceans. Some of the salt was carried to the oceans by rivers that started far inland. And some of it came from the shells and skeletons of sea animals. It took hundreds of millions of years for the oceans to become as salty as they are today.

From a distance, the ocean's surface looks smooth, flat, and featureless. The ocean floor, however, is far different. If you could magically dry up all the oceans, you would see a fantastic world of valleys, plateaus, canyons, gorges, mountains, and trenches.

In many places at the edge of the continents, the land beneath the ocean has a gentle downward slope. This is called the *continental shelf*. In a way, it is like a ribbon wrapped around the continent. In some places, this shelf is very narrow, extending less than a mile from the shore. In other places, it is many miles wide.

The water over the continental shelf is shallow compared to the water in other parts of the ocean. For example, at its deepest points, the water of the continental shelf would just about cover the top of the Empire State Building. But at the deepest part of the Pacific Ocean, the water is thirty times as deep!

At the edge of the continental shelf, there is a sharp drop in the ocean floor. This area, where the ocean depth increases sharply, is called the *continental slope*. It is not smooth, like the continental shelf. Instead, it is rough and jagged, cut by huge canyons and gorges.

At its base, the continental slope meets a fairly flat ocean floor called the *abyssal plain*. Abyssal comes from the word *abyss*, which means "bottomless pit." Of course, the abyssal plain isn't bottomless, but it is far beneath the surface of the ocean.

The floors of the abyssal plains are covered by thick layers of mud, sand, and the skeletons and shells of dead plants and animals. Underneath these layers is hard rock, called basalt. Underwater currents smooth out the sediment—or accumulated mud, sand, and shells—the way surface waves smooth a sandy beach.

The abyssal plains do not stretch from one continent to another, even though they do make up most of the ocean's floor. The abyssal plains are broken by massive underwater mountain ranges. The Mid-Atlantic Ridge is a long mountain range that snakes down the center of the Atlantic Ocean.

Most of the mountains that rise from the ocean's floor are so far underwater that we cannot see them. But some are so tall that their peaks poke above the surface of the water. Iceland, in the North Atlantic, and the Azores, which are islands in the mid-Atlantic, are parts of the Mid-Atlantic Ridge.

There are also ridges in the Pacific Ocean. The Pacific Ridge rises above the surface of the ocean in a number of places. The Hawaiian Islands are examples of volcanic mountains that are part of the Pacific Ridge. The canyons of the Pacific Ridge are far deeper than those in the Atlantic.

The Marianas Trench, in the western Pacific Ocean, is the deepest known place in the ocean. If Mount Everest—the tallest mountain in the world—could be placed at the bottom of the Marianas Trench, its peak would still be more than a mile below the surface of the ocean!

There is a great deal of activity going on in the depths of the oceans—volcanoes erupt, the ocean floor shifts, and earthquakes frequently occur. An earthquake under the ocean can create an enormous wave, called a *tsunami*.

A tsunami is a long wave that moves almost as fast as a jet plane. When the tsunami reaches the shoreline, it may build up as tall as a ten-story building. The force of such a wave is terrible. It crashes down on the land, smashing everything in its path.

Tsunamis are sometimes called tidal waves, but they have nothing to do with the ocean's tides. Tides are simply the daily rise and fall of the ocean's waters. Every day there are two high tides and two low tides, caused mainly by the gravitational pull of the moon.

The moon's gravity pulls the ocean water, making it bulge out. This is the high tide. Where the water is not bulging out, it is low tide. Since the Earth is constantly spinning and presenting a different part of its surface to the moon, the tides keep rising and falling, rising and falling.

Besides the tides, water in the ocean also moves in a different way—it moves in streams called *currents.* Some currents move along the surface, while others flow deep down in the ocean. Some are warm currents, while others are colder.

The Gulf Stream is a warm current that

starts in the Gulf of Mexico, runs up the east coast of North America, then across the Atlantic Ocean to Europe. Seen from an airplane, the Gulf Stream looks like a light, blue-green streak across a dark-blue background.

Currents are important to sea life. For example, the Humboldt Current, a cold current that runs north along the west coast of South America, is full of minerals. These minerals are food for countless millions of tiny plants and animals called plankton. Fish of all sizes and kinds follow this current to feed on the rich supplies of plankton. And human beings, in turn, have great success fishing in the waters of the Humboldt Current.

Except in their very deepest parts, the oceans are teeming with plants and animals, which are linked together in a huge food chain. At the bottom of the food chain are plankton and microscopic plants called algae. They serve as food for small and large fish, and shellfish such as clams, mussels, and oysters that live on the ocean floor.

In turn, these are food for the larger fish, and so on. Some of the largest ocean dwellers, however—the blue whales—eat nothing but microscopic plankton!

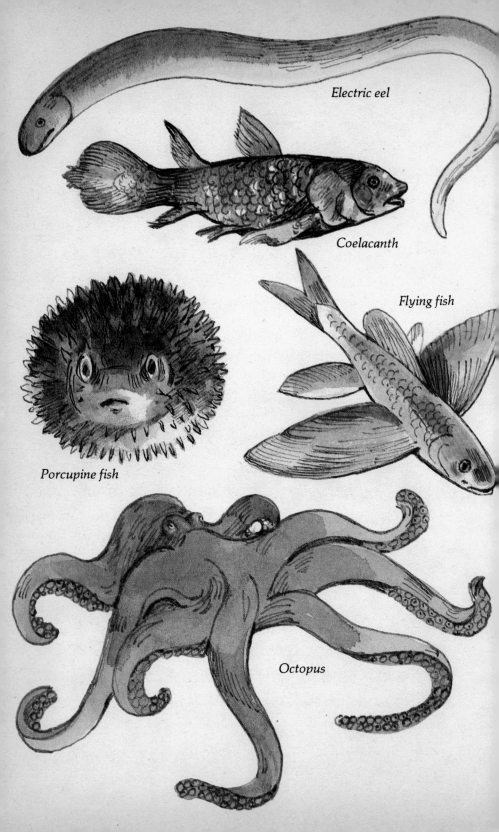

Electric eel

Coelacanth

Flying fish

Porcupine fish

Octopus

The ocean is home to many strange and unusual creatures. There is the electric eel, that glows in the darkness of the ocean depths, and the flying fish, that can soar above the water as high as a two-story house. There is the porcupine fish, which is covered with sharp, bony needles, and the octopus, with its eight long, whiplike tentacles.

There is even a creature in the ocean that was thought to have disappeared millions of years ago. It is called the *coelacanth*. This weird-looking, bony fish is like a living fossil. It is a member of the same family from which all reptiles, birds, and mammals evolved.

As the sea gave rise to all the life forms on Earth today, so it continues to enrich our world. It supplies us with food. The ocean water that evaporates into the air falls on the land as much-needed rain and snow. The plants growing in the oceans give off oxygen that is needed by animals of all kinds.

Every day, we use the oceans for shipping, for fishing, and for travel. And now we are looking to the ocean to supply us with oil and minerals to replace what we have taken from the land.

The uses of the ocean are endless. And we are only beginning to learn how rich and amazing is the vast blue world of the ocean.